Fall Fun

Charity Alexander

DEDICATION

To my granddaughter—who has so much fun in the fall.

pumpkin

THIS IS A PUMPKIN. IT'S ORANGE AND ROUND. IT'S GROWN IN A GARDEN AND SITS ON THE GROUND.

apple

THE APPLE IS A YUMMY
TREAT. I LOVE IT'S CRUNCH,
CRUNCH, CRUNCH WHEN I
EAT.

leaf

THE LEAVES CHANGE COLORS AND FALL ON THE GROUND. IT'S SO MUCH FUN TO PICK ONE UP AND TAKE IT HOME!

trees

OH, HOW BEAUTIFUL ARE THE TREES! THEY TURN YELLOW AND RED AND ORANGE.

squirrel

THE SQUIRREL IS VERY BUSY IN THE FALL. HE HAS TO COLLECT ALL HIS FOOD FOR THE WINTER.

Indian corn

INDIAN CORN MAKES A NICE DECORATION. SEE ALL THE WONDERFUL COLORS?

acorn

THE ACORNS ARE FALLING FROM THE TREES. IT IS A GOOD THING, SOON THE SQUIRREL WILL GATHER THEM UP TO EAT.

turkey

THE TURKEY SAYS "GOBBLE, GOBBLE" AND WADDLES AROUND. LOOK AT THE BIG FEATHERS ON HIS TAIL!

haystack

THE FARMER IS GATHERING ALL THE HAY. CAN YOU FIND THE NEEDLE IN THE HAYSTACK?

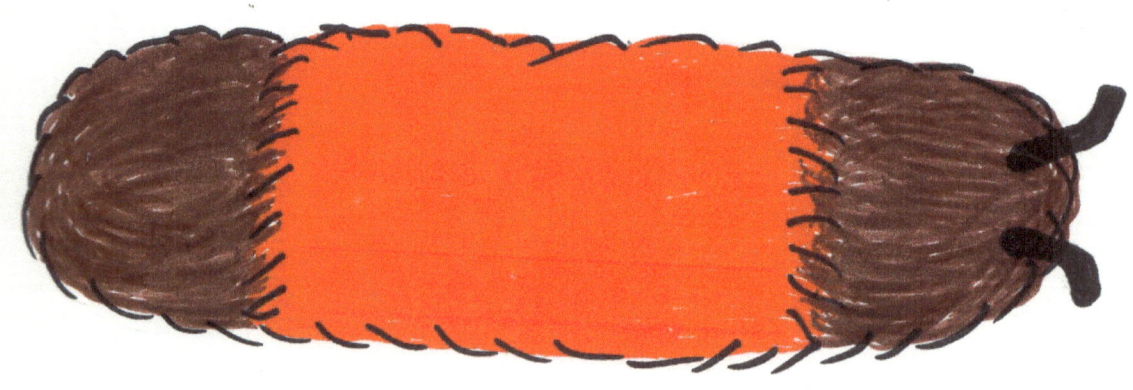

woolly worm

THE WOOLLY WORM IS SOFT AND FUZZY. HE EATS AND EATS AND EATS TO GET READY TO GO INTO HIS COCOON FOR THE WINTER. IN THE SPRING HE WILL TURN INTO A BEAUTIFUL BUTTERFLY!

ABOUT THE AUTHOR

Charity Alexander is a teacher, author, and nurse—but most of all a mother and grandmother. One of her favorite times is story-time with little Sari.

www.ingramcontent.com/pod-product-compliance
Lightning Source LLC
Chambersburg PA
CBHW060822290526
45792CB00005BB/1764